CASIAN ANTON (born July 30, 1988) private analyst in International Relations with concerns in the study of interdisciplinary methodology, world state and structures of explanation. QTS in Humanities (2016 in England, 2011 in Romania, Petru Maior's University of Târgu Mureş), MA in *Security and International Relations* ('Lucian Blaga' University of Sibiu, Romania, 2013), BA in *International Relations and European Studies* (Petru Maior's University of Târgu Mureş, Romania, 2011), Erasmus Student to *University of Social Science and Humanities* (Warsaw, Poland, 2012-2013).

Series *Papers in International Relations:*

1. The Concept and the Meaning of I(i)nternational R(r)elations.

Hi,

I'm Casian. I hope my gift finds you well.

I'm glad that you decided to take a chance with me and read this research. & I hope my method of writing and thinking will enlighten your mind about this topic.

This edition is a signed gift to charity to be sold at their own discretion. Thank you for purchasing this short research book.

Best wishes,
Casian, October 24, 2022

[signature]
Octobre 25, 2022
Luton

The Concept *and* the Meaning *of* I(i)nternational R(r)elations

Casian Anton

Revi Project 88

Author: Casian Anton
Cover: Apple Pages
Translated into English: Casian Anton, Maria Macovei
Series: *Papers in International Relations*

Printed by Amazon

"The Concept *and* the Meaning *of* I(i)nternational R(r)elations"

ISBN: 9798846527775

Revi Project 88 (London, UK): *is dedicated to create knowledge and advance the understanding of various topics in the field of Humanities (International Relations as a specific area of study). All the activities within this project is to guide, exchange, sustain and share unique and original ideas that can help people to understand the world.*

Online orders: www.amazon.com
Contact: www.reviproject88.com
Social Media: Revi Project 88 (Twitter, Facebook, Instagram, Tumblr)

SECOND EDITION

Table of Contents

HOW TO READ AND UNDERSTAND THE RESEARCH

In this chapter I offered a brief explanation of the method of reading and understanding of the research available in this short book.

Each paragraph in each chapter starts with *Number 1* and continues, depending on the explanations provided and the researched topics, with *Number 1.1* or starts with *2*, *3* or *4* and so forth.

Number 1 = is the main idea.

Number 1.1 = continues the main idea written in 1, but at a more in-depth level, in the sense that it provides the etymological roots and examples of the main idea.

Number 1.1.1 continues to provide in-depth information of the etymological roots and examples (if available) written in *Number 1.1*.

Number 1.1.1 supports and continues the etymological roots and examples of the information written in *Number 1.1*.

Number 1.2, *1.3* or *1.4* is the second, third or fourth part (where there is the possibility to provide explanations in several parts) of the main idea written in *Number 1*.

More numbers after *Number 1*, for example: *1.2.2.1.1.1*, mean a deeper level of meaning, of the etymological roots and examples of the main idea.

In short:

1 = the main idea

1.1 = the first more in-depth explanation of the main idea.

1.1.1 = even more in-depth explanation of the idea from *1.1*, but strongly connected with the idea written in *Number 1.*

1.2 = the second more in-depth explanation of the main idea in *Number 1*.

1.2.1.1.1.1 = the most in-depth level of explanations of the main idea.

2 = the second main idea.

After *Number 2*, the process written above is repeated (*Number 3, Number 4, Number 5 ...*) until all the main ideas of the research paper were explored and the research is finished.

INTRODUCTION

1. After the end of the Cold War and the global Internet revolution, the concept of 'international relations' began to be used intensively in the public space. It became so popular that it passed the academic debating borders or the foreign policy news section. On Google there are more than a billion results for 'international relations'.[1]

2. Today, 'I(i)nternational R(r)elations' has two meanings which are given by the following examples:

(i) „International Relations is the study of the relations among states and other political and economic units in the international system."[2]

---

[1] "international relations," Google, last accessed: August 14, 2022.
[2] "international relations," Infoplease, last accessed: June 20, 2015,
http://www.infoplease.com/encyclopedia/history/international-relations.html.

(ii) „The political relationships that exist between different countries (MacMillan Dictionary)."[3]

2.1 Another form of writing this concept exists when in some books and articles 'I(i)nternational R(r)elations' is written with lowercase and in others with uppercase:

(i) „After 1970s the international relations between the US and China began to improve. Following a meeting between the two presidents, both parties agreed to sign an economic cooperation treaty;"

(ii) „International Relations (IR) is uneasy about its status as a 'science'"[4]

(iii) „[...] or the implications of human security paradigm for the study and practice of international relations;"[5]

---

[3] "international relations," MacMillan Dictionary, last accessed: June 20, 2015,
http://www.macmillandictionary.com/dictionary/british/internationaI-relations.

[4] Nuno P. Monterio, Keven G. Ruby, "IR and the False Promise of Philosophical Foundations," *International Theory* 1 (2009): 16, last accessed: July 2, 2012, doi: 10.1017/S1752971909000050.

[5] Leucea Ioana, *Constructivism şi securitate umană*, (Iaşi: Editura Institutul European, 2012): 13.

(iv) „International Relations (RI) has always had anti-theorists;"[6]

(v) „This fact has radically changed the regulatory principle of international relations, from power politics of the European system to a politics of cooperation;"[7]

3. Scholars agree that 'I(i)nternational R(r)elations' does not have a universal accepted concept and the current ones are general, which offers a reduced analytic utility.

4. In this paper I explored the concept of 'I(i)nternational R(r)elations', with the aim (i) to show the two techniques of writing and their representation, (ii) the meaning that is attached to each technique; (iii) the process of creation of a concept based on two terms.

4.1 The two techniques are: two versions of the concept of 'I(i)nternational R(r)elations': (i) the ad litteram or literally concept and (ii) the scientific concept; two meanings of the concept I(i)nternational R(r)elations: (i) when it is written

---

[6] Christian Reus Smith, "International Relations, Irrelevant? Don't Blame Theory," *Millenium - Journal of International Studies* 40 (2012): 525, last accessed: July 18, 2012, doi: 10.1177/0305829812442046.

[7] Andrei Miroiu, "Evoluţia sistemului internaţional după 1914," în Andrei Miroiu, Radu-Sebastian Ungureanu (editori), *Manual de relaţii internaţionale*, (Iaşi: Editura Polirom, 2006): 31.

with lowercase 'international relations' and when it is written with uppercase 'International Relations,' abbreviated IR.

4.1.1 The scientific concept is built from the ad litteram/literally concept + the scope of science + the operating process of the inter-discipline.

4.1.1.1 The scientific concept, however, does not remove the general view of the concept, but it is good because it can show the differences between the two techniques of writing and their meaning.

4.1.1.2 Furthermore, by using the ad litteram/literally concept + the scope of science + the operating process of the inter-discipline, I will build three scientific concepts based on the research interests of the IR inter-discipline. These three concepts eliminate the general view of the concept, but only from the point of view of the three concepts and research interests.

4.1.2 The ad litteram or literal concept is constructed from the union of the two terms 'relation' and 'international'.

5. Through this paper: (i) I return to theorizing the concept of 'I(i)nternational R(r)elations' but from its etymological bases; (ii) the terms 'relation' and 'international' is based on a wide range of concepts that help its formation, and I want to *show this formation*; (iii) I contribute to the existing literature that discusses the concept; (iv) I contribute to the historical development of the interdiscipline and (v) I respond to the crisis of ideas in science.

5.1 To show the process of creation, how a concept looks like and its elements, I used the writing model of the Austrian-British philosopher Ludwig Wittgenstein, from his book *Tractatus Logico-Philosophicus*[8] and of the English philosopher Thomas Hobbes from his book *The Elements of Law - Natural and Politic.*[9]

6. The paper is organized as follows: I started with (i) defining the concept, and (ii) the meaning, then (iii) I explored the concept and the meaning of 'I(i)nternational R(r)elations', and (iv) in *Conclusions* I returned to the scope of the paper and I addressed the process of creating a concept.

7. If you started reading this paper it means that it is time to look with greater clarity and objectivity to all the elements and the process of creating a concept. To *see* the concept of 'I(i)nternational R(r)elations' *as it is.*

---

[8] Ludwig Wittgenstein, *Tractatus Logico-Philosophicus*, First Edition (London: Routledge, 2013), Kindle.
[9] Thomas Hobbes, *The Elements of Law - Natural and Politic*, (USA: CreateSpace Independent Publishing Platform, 2015).

WHAT IS 'CONCEPT'?

1. Ironically, the very term[10] 'concept' has no universal accepted definition.

1.1 Furthermore, due to the theoretical difficulty of creating a universally accepted concept, the definition of 'concept' has several versions, which can create a terminological confusion.[11]

2. As regards the construction of a 'concept,' in the mainstream literature there are two groups: (i) the objectivists who say that concepts exist independently of the individual's mind and (ii) the

---

[10] In this paper I use 'term' instead of 'word.' A 'word' is a set of letters that combined and modified form a sentence, it is a language component. A 'term' is a word that has sense, and refers to an event, relation, idea, object, etc. 'Term' is a point of reference, 'word' is component of the language. All 'terms' can be 'words' but not all 'words' can be 'terms.' 'International' and 'relations' are 'words' and 'terms.'

[11] William McDougall, "The Confusion of the Concept," *Journal of Philosophical Studies* 3 (1928): 427, last accessed: July 31, 2015, http://www.jstor.org/stable/3745675.

subjectivists who claim that concepts are mental phenomena, i.e. in the mind or head of the individual.[12]

3. However, the current literature provides several definitions.

3.1 The concept is:

(i) a general idea;

(ii) a model of presentation;

(iii) a model showing us how we think about objects;

(iv) a general theory of knowledge;

(v) includes a broader understanding of a short term;

(vi) establish a meaning that says more than it seems;
(vii) identifies the elements that a term has;

(viii) distinguishes between a lot of other terms;

---

[12] Hans-Johann Glock, "Concepts: Where Subjectivism Goes Wrong," *Philosophy* 84 (2009): 5-6, last accessed: May 2, 2014, doi: 10.1017/S0031819109000011.

(ix) a theoretical construction that facilitates application of the concept in practice[13].

4. Paul Thagard writes an incomplete list, in his words, about the roles that a concept has: classification, learning, memorising, explaining and generalizing.[14]

5. There are accepted, contested and rejected concepts.

5.1 *The accepted concepts* are named universal concepts: everyone uses the meaning attached to the concept without regret.

5.2 *The challenged concepts*: do not give a sufficiently clear meaning and often causes a terminological confusion among scholars and other readers.

6. There is a possibility where a concept is accepted by some specialists and challenged or rejected by others.

7. The concept of 'I(i)nternational R(r)elations' is misleading, general and contested by researchers. It is found in all roles written by Paul Thagard.

---

[13] *Ibidem*, 5.
[14] The other roles are in Paul Thagard, "Concepts and Conceptual Change," *Synthese* 82 (1990): 258-259, last accessed: July 31, 2015, http://www.jstor.org/stable/20116749.

WHAT IS 'MEANING'?

1. From my research I did not find sources saying that 'meaning' may or may not have a universally accepted concept, is contested or rejected.

2. According to online dictionaries, 'meaning' is:

(i) the semantic content of a word, significance, sense;[15]

(i.i) 'semantics' is a „branch of linguistics that deals with the study of meanings of words and the evolution of those meanings;"[16]

(ii) that which is intended to be or is, expression, indication;[17]

---

[15] "semnificaţie," Dexonline.ro, last accessed: June 20, 2015, https://dexonline.ro/definitie/semnifica%C8%9Bie.
[16] "semantic," Dexonline.ro, last accessed: June 20, 2015, https://dexonline.ro/definitie/semantic.
[17] "meaning," Dictionary.com, last accessed: June 20, 2015, http://dictionary.reference.com/browse/meaning?s=t.

(iii) what is expressed or represented;[18]

(iv) the idea represented by the word or the phrase;[19]

(v) the idea that a person wants to express.[20]

3. In this case, I(i)nternational R(r)elations can be written in two ways: (i) when is written with lowercase 'international relations' and (ii) when is written with uppercase 'International Relations,' shortened IR.

3.1 As regards the two ways of writing, they are used in I(i)nternational R(r)elations literature, but most often, as happens in the Romanian literature, with the same sense or interchangeably: discipline, inter-discipline and domain of study. Yet, some texts do not mention anything about discipline, inter-discipline and domain of study. This situation contributes to the terminological confusion.

---

[18] "meaning," Cambridge Dictionary Online, last accessed: June 20, 2015,
http://dictionary.cambridge.org/dictionary/english/meaning.
[19] "meaning," Merriam-Webster, last accessed: June 20, 2015,
http://www.merriam-webster.com/dictionary/meaning.
[20] *Ibidem*.

THE CONCEPT AND THE MEANING OF I(i)NTERNATIONAL R(r)ELATIONS

1. The term[21] 'relation,' according to the *Online Etymology Dictionary*, has been used since the late 14 c..[22]

2. The term 'international' first appeared, according to *Online Etymology Dictionary*[23] and in the article written by Hidemi Suganami,[24] in a book written by the English philosopher and jurist

---

[21] 'Relation' and 'international' are 'words' and 'terms.' For the rest of the paper I will use 'international' and 'relation' as 'terms.'
[22] "relation," Online Etymology Dictionary, last accessed: June 20, 2015,
http://www.etymonline.com/index.php?allowed_in_frame=0&search=relation&searchmode=none.
[23] "international," Online Etymology Dictionary, last accessed: June 20, 2015,
http://www.etymonline.com/index.php?allowed_in_frame=0&search=international&searchmode=none.
[24] Hidemi Suganami, "A Note on the Origin of the Word 'International,'" *British Journal of International Studies* 4 (1978): 226 - 232, last accessed: June 26, 2015, doi: 10.1017/S0260210500114585.

Jeremy Bentham, *An Introduction to the Principles of Morals and Legislation*, published in 1789.

2.1 Information about the term 'international' is found in footnote '143':

„**143.** The word[25] *international,* it must be acknowledged, is a new one; although, it is hoped, sufficiently analogous and intelligible. It is calculated to express, in a significant way, the branch of law which goes commonly under the name of the *law of nations:* a name so unusual that, were it not for the force of custom, it would seem rather to refer to internal jurisprudence.”[26]

2.1.1 In footnote '143' Jeremy Bentham writes a definition of 'international' which is not so clear but it can become more clear if I cut a few sentences:

„The word *international* [...] a name so unusual that, were it not for the force of custom, it would seem rather to refer to internal jurisprudence.”[27]

---

[25] Jeremy Bentham uses 'word' instead of 'term,' but as I said in footnote *12*, 'international' is a 'word' and a 'term.' I decided to used it as a 'term' because it represents something.

[26] Jeremy Bentham, *An Introduction to the Principles of Morals and Legislation*, (1789). In this paper I used the edition published in 1823, available online: http://oll.libertyfund.org/titles/278 (last accessed: June 20, 2015).

[27] *Ibidem.*

2.1.2 In the next footnote, '144,' Jeremy Bentham writes about the term 'international' in a manner which can be considered as a concept of 'international:'

> „if the dispute had been betwixt Philip [the IIIrd of Spain - added by author] and James [the Ist of England - added by author] himself, it would have been international."[28]

3. I(i)nternational R(r)elations:

3.1 'Relations' means ties, connections, correspondences, reports between things, facts, people, ideas, processes and events.[29]

3.2 'International' is composed of two terms: 'inter' and 'national.'

3.2.1 'Inter' is used as a compounding element meaning 'between.'[30]

3.2.2 'National' refers to 'nation' and 'state.'[31]

---

[28] *Ibidem.*

[29] "relation," The Free Dictionary by Farlex, accessed June 20, 2015, http://www.thefreedictionary.com/relation; "relation," Dictionary.com, last accessed: June 20, 2015, http://dictionary.reference.com/browse/relation;

[30] "inter," Dictionary.com, last accessed: June 20, 2015, http://dictionary.reference.com/browse/inter?s=t.

[31] "naţional," Dictionary.com, last accessed: June 20, 2015, http://dictionary.reference.com/browse/national?s=t; "Dex.ro,"

3.2.2.1 'Nation'[32] is a human stable community that shares, to a great extent, a common history, common language, common culture, common religion[33] and population in a given geographical area.[34]

3.2.2.2 'State'[35] is a supra-structural institution recognized by most existing states with defined geographical borders, stable population, the population obeys the laws and constitution (they are the basic texts that establish rights and obligations for the citizens of the state - it is voted by population: 50% + 1 and valid for the entire population: 100%).[36]

3.2.2.2.1 The state represents legally, and in the inside and outside of its geographical borders, the nation.

---

național, last accessed: June 20, 2015, https://www.dex.ro/național.

[32] There is no accepted concept.

[33] Karen A. Mingst, *Essentials of International Relations*, Second Edition, (London, New York: W.W Norton & Company, 2003): 100.

[34] The concept of nation that does not reflect reality. The 'common' is used because of the democratic system: if in a group of humans 50% + 1% uses the same language or religion, that language and religion will become the 'common' language and religion.

[35] There is no accepted concept.

[36] Karen A. Mingst, *Essentials,* 100-102.

23

3.2.2.2.2 The state is based on the principle of separation of powers: legislative, executive and judicial.

3.2.2.2.3 The state is a human community that recognizes only one government on its territory.

3.2.2.2.4 The state is recognized by other states.

3.2.2.2.5 The population inside the state forms the civil society.

3.2.2.2.6 The state is a sum of institutions that applies laws and collects taxes.

3.2.2.2.6.1 These institutions form the public administration body, which means all institutions of a state.

3.2.2.2.6.1.1 In public administration there is an institution different from other public administration institutions that is subordinated to the government – i.e. the central institution for exercising the executive power of the state (the executive power) - and is used in order to start and maintain relations with nations and states. The name of this institution, among world states, is the 'Ministry of Foreign Affairs.'

3.2.2.2.7 The components or the elements forming the State are: the form of government:[37] monarchy (absolute, constitutional, dualist) or republic (parliamentary, presidential, semi-presidential, directorial, mixed) and theocracy; religion (e.g.: Judaism, Catholicism, Confucianism, Buddhism, Hinduism, Atheism); economics (free, state-controlled, mixed); population (black skin, yellow skin, white skin or Negroid, Mongoloid, Caucasoid also named Europid); culture (e.g.: ways of thinking, values, rules, symbols, clothing, art, music, kitchen); environmental: abiotic (relief, air, water, soil), biotic (plants and animals) and human (with their activities).

3.2.2.2.8 In literature 'state' is known and used also with/under the name 'state actor.'

4. Based on deciphering each term from point **1.** to **3.,** we have the following **ad litteram concept/literally** concept, is what each term means and their reunion in one formula and use: international relations are ties, connections, correspondences, reports of things, facts, ideas, processes and events *between* nations and states and their components/elements: forms of government: monarchy (absolute, constitutional, dualist) or republic (parliamentary, presidential, semi-presidential, directorial, mixed) and

---

[37] It refers to mode of how executive power is organized in a state: how it is elected and gain legitimacy as head of state.

theocracy; religion (e.g.: Judaism, Catholicism, Confucianism, Buddhism, Hinduism, Atheism); economics (free, state-controlled, mixed); population (black skin, yellow skin, white skin or Negroid, Mongoloid, Caucasoid also named Europid); culture (e.g.: ways of thinking, values, rules, symbols, clothing, art, music, kitchen); environmental: abiotic (relief, air, water, soil), biotic (plants and animals) and humans (with their activities).

4.1 There are connections between nations, states and multinational companies (shortened MNC, henceforth MNC, like Facebook, Google, Microsoft), transnational companies (shortened TNC, henceforth TNC, like General Electric, Toyota, Nestlè), international governmental and intergovernmental organizations (shortened IGO, henceforth IGO, like European Union or United Nations) and international non-governmental organizations (shortened NGO, henceforth NGO - like Transparency International or Amnesty International).

4.1.1 Although they do not appear *per se* in the ad litteram/literally concept, MNCs, TNCs, IGOs and NGOs are *inside* the concept, more precisely, in the elements of the concept and based on their activity: politics, economics, religion and so forth.

4.1.1.1 In order for a MNC, TNC, IGO and a NGO to conduct a business or project in a state, the state, by its institutions and laws, agree their activity on its territory and population.

4.1.2 In the mainstream literature, 'MNC', 'TNC', 'IGO' and 'NGO' are known and used with/under the name 'non state actor.'

5. International relations are established through treaties, conventions, agreements, and contracts.

5.1 Also, treaties, conventions, agreements and contracts can exist between states and MNCs, TNCs, IGOs and NGOs.

6. There are two types of international relations:

6.1 *Bilateral relations*: between two state or non-state actors.

6.2 *Multilateral relations*: between at least three state or non-state actors.

7. In the next section I will develop the aim of the article written in *Introduction*: the two techniques of writing and the representation of the concept, plus the meaning attached to each technique: (i) the ad litteram/literally concept and (ii) the scientific concept. The two meanings of the concept of I(i)nternational R(r)elations: (i) the meaning when it is written with lowercase 'international relations' and (ii) when the meaning is written with uppercase 'International Relations'.

7.1 Written with **lowercase** 'international relations' in general refers to:

(i) the ad litteram/literally concept;

(ii) when we shorten the information. Instead of enumerating all types of relations between nations and states (economic, political, environmental, cultural and so forth) scholars select the easiest way: a combination of terms that comprises all of them.

7.2 Written with **uppercase** 'International Relations' (shortened IR, henceforth IR) in general refers to 'science' (here is also the scientific concept), the 'inter-discipline' and 'specialization' of International Relations, shortened IR.[38]

---

[38] For example see: Monterio și Ruby, "IR and the False Promise," 16; Christian Reus Smith, "International Relations, Irrelevant?," 525; George Lawson, "The Eternal Divide? History and International Relations," *European Journal of International Relations* 18 (2010): 203, last accessed: June 28, 2012, doi: 10.1177/1354066110373561; Hidemi Suganami, "Narrative Explanation and International Relations: Back to Basics," *Millenium - Journal of International Studies* 37 (2008): 2, last accessed: July 18, 2012, doi: 10.1177/0305829808097643; Joshua

7.2.2 'Science'[39] is a human effort to understand the objective and subjective reality.

7.2.2.1 Science begins when a researcher/person has a question: "Why it rains?" or "What are clouds made of?"

7.2.2.1.1 To find the answer, a scholar/person (i) uses a scientific method and (ii) collects particular data on the subject investigated.

7.2.2.2 The scope of science is to study, to research, to respond and to explain the question asked by the curious scholar who wants an answer by using scientific methods and by collecting particular data.

7.2.2.3 The result differ in essence.

7.2.2.3.1 This essence consists in (i) accepting, contesting or rejecting the results and (ii) using scientific methods: sometimes to find the same answer, a scholar uses a method and another scholar uses another method. It is possible for both scholars to have the same results or not.

S. Goldstein and Jon C. Pevehouse, *International Relations, 2013-2014 Update*, Tenth Edition, (London: Pearson, 2013): 3.
[39] There is no accepted concept.

7.2.3 To understand 'inter-discipline' we must first see what 'discipline' is.

7.2.3.1 'Discipline' is a common body of methods, ways of investigation, and exchange of results.

7.2.3.1.1 All the disciplines create a common body of knowledge, theories, laws, norms and values.

7.2.3.2 'Inter' is used as a compounding element meaning 'between.'[40]

7.2.3.3 'Inter-discipline'[41] combines, merges, brings research methodologies, concepts, bodies of knowledge, thinking patterns, ideas and particular data from at least two disciplines in order to find new information on a subject of research.

---

[40] "inter," Dictionary.com.

[41] There is no accepted concept. Melissa Miles, Sarah Rainbird, "Evaluating Interdisciplinary Collaborative Learning and Assessment in the Creative Arts and Humanities," *Arts & Humanities in Higher Education*, Online First (2014): 2, last accessed: February 3, 2015, doi: 10.1177/1474022214561759; Jian Qin, F. W. Lancaster, Bryce Allen, "Types and Levels of Collaboration in Interdisciplinary Research in the Sciences," *Journal of the American Society for Information Science* 48 (1997): 893, last accessed: February 4, 2015, doi: 10.1002/(SICI)1097-4571(199710)48:10<893::AID-ASI5>3.0.CO;2-X.

7.2.3.3.1 From a discipline, particular data are taken into consideration that combined with other particular data can produce new information unknown to researchers.

7.2.3.3.2 The new piece of information must be applied universally.[42]

7.2.3.3.3 The result is different in essence.

7.2.3.3.3.1 This essence consists of (i) accepting, contesting or rejecting the results and (ii) using scientific methods: sometimes to find the same answer, a researcher uses a method and another researcher uses another method. It is possible for both researchers have the same results or not.

7.2.4 In order to better understand the IR inter-discipline, I will also define 'domain of study.'

---

[42] Kevyn Yong, Stephen J. Sauer, Elizabeth A. Mannix, "Conflict and Creativity in Interdisciplinary Teams," *Small Group Research* 45 (2014): 267, last accessed: February 2, 2015, doi: 10.1177/1046496414530789; Moti Nissani, "Fruits, Salads, and Smoothies: A Working Definition of Interdisciplinarity," *The Journal of Educational Thought (JET) / Revue de la Pensée Éducative* 29 (1995): 121-122, last accessed: February 6, 2015, http://www.jstor.org/stable/23767672?seq=1#page_scan_tab_co ntents; Arianne Abell Walker, "Interdisciplinary Studies in the Community Colleges," *New Directions for Community Colleges* 108 (1999): 50, last accessed: February 6, 2015, doi: 10.1002/cc.10805.

7.2.4.1 'Domain of study' is a sector, a sphere of activity in which intellectual work is carried out to acquire a thorough knowledge about specific subjects of interest.

7.2.4.1.1 'International Relations' is found under the study domain known as 'Social Science,' 'Global Studies,' 'International Studies' and 'Political Science.' Depends from one country to another.

7.2.4.1.1.1 'International Relations' is one of the branches/specializations of the 'Social Science,' 'Global Studies,' 'International Studies' and 'Political Science' domain of study.

7.2.5 'Specialization' means to learn, to dedicate to a branch of activity from a domain of study in order to become a 'specialist.'

7.2.5.1 'Specialist' is a person with very good knowledge in a branch of activity/specialization of a domain of study.

7.2.5.1.1 The knowledge will be used by a specialist to fulfill the scope of the branch of activity/specialization from the domain of study.

7.3 In some situations 'International Relations' replaces the term 'History.'

7.3.1 Most often the replacement applies to university courses and book titles: *International Relations after 1914*, *International Relations 1700 - 1800*, *International Relations 1800 - 1900*, *International Relations in the Twentieth Century (XX)*, *International Relations: USA and USSR (1970-1980)*, *International Relations after the Cold War* or any title that uses 'International Relations' and years in (i) Arabic numerals (1600, 1914) or (ii) Roman numerals (referring to centuries: XVII, XVIII, , XX, XXI).

7.3.1.1 Although the title of the course, article or book includes the terms 'International Relations,' the text is neither about the history of how 'science,' 'inter-discipline' and 'specialization' was formed from 1600 to 1700, or after the Cold War, nor the new scientific approaches between 1800 - 1900 or after the Cold War, but it is a course, article or a book which discusses the most important events that occurred after 1914, 1700-1800, 1800-1900 or after the Cold War. In other words, is history written by historians. The history and the formation of the 'inter-discipline', 'specialization' or the new scientific discoveries are discussed in courses, articles and books like *Introduction in International Relations* and *Theory of International Relations*. It is usually specified in the *Introduction* of the course, article or book about the nature and objective of the text: history, theory of IR interdisciplinary, or a combination of the two.

7.3.2 Another reason why 'International Relations' is replaced with 'History', even if it is unfair to history and historians, and not at all malicious - history, after George Lawson,[43] is the central locomotive of the inter-discipline - is to form a specialization in universities, which, at the level of image, to identify with the specialization title. To look more homogenous. In fact, based on the content of courses and books, the titles of *International Relations after 1914*, *International Relations 1700-1800*, *International Relations 1800-1900, International Relations in the Twentieth Century (XX)*, are synonymous with the titles *History after 1914*, *History from 1700-1800*, *History from 1800-1900* and *History of the Twentieth Century (XX)*.

7.3.2.1 This situation, however, does not exist in all universities. On some courses with the title *International Relations after 1914* or *International Relations after the Cold War*, or any title that uses 'International Relations' and years in Arabic or Roman numerals, events from history are discussed but from the point of view of the concepts and theories which 'inter-discipline' and 'specialization' use to explain that historic event

---

[43] George Lawson, "The Eternal Divide?" 205.

(e.g.: realism, neo-realism, polarity, power, national interest, security).

7.3.2.1.1 In order to observe the differences of writing, the meaning behind it and how misleading are the ways of writing, I return to the examples from *Introduction*. For each example I will write what is the meaning in terms of: ad litteram/literally concept or science (the scientific concept), inter-discipline and specialization of IR.

(i) „After 1970s, the international relations between USA and China began to improve. Following a meeting between the two presidents, both parties agreed to sign an economic cooperation treaty:" it *refers to ad litteram/literally concept and shortens the information;*

(ii) „International Relations (IR) is uneasy about its status as a 'science'"[44]: *it refers to science (the scientific concept), inter-discipline and specialization of IR;*

(iii) „[...] or the implications of human security paradigm for the study and practice of international relations:"[45] *it refers to science (the scientific concept), inter-discipline and specialization of IR;*

---

[44] Monterio and Ruby, "IR and the False Promise," 16.

[45] Leucea Ioana, *Constructivism*, 13.

(iii.i) „[...] the practice of international relations" falls into the 'science' and 'inter-discipline' of IR because in practice, i.e. diplomatic meetings, political conferences, civil society, an IR specialist is using using the knowledge of the science (the scientific concept) and inter-discipline of IR;

(iv) „International Relations (IR) has always had anti-theorists:"[46] *it refers to science (the scientific concept), inter-discipline and specialization of IR;*

(v) „This fact has radically changed the regulatory principle of international relations, from power politics of the European system to a politics of cooperation:"[47] *it refers to the ad litteram/literally concept and shortens the information.*

7.3.2.2 Curious readers and students will learn about the true meaning of the concept I(i)nternational R(r)elations (add litteram or science) in the following situations:

(i) while participating to a course and observe that discussions are about an event from history or science;

(ii) while reading a book and observe that the information is about an historical event or about

---

[46] Christian Reus Smith, "International Relations, Irrelevant?," 525.
[47] Andrei Miroiu, "Evoluţia sistemului," 31.

the science, inter-discipline and specialization of IR; there are many books and articles which do not mention anything about the meaning of the concept and, therefore, is in the eye of the reader to decide and understand what the author might refer to;

(ii.i) in their paper, Monterio and Ruby write about what they refer to: „[...] we use 'IR' to refer to the discipline of International Relations and 'international relations' to refer to its substantive domain of study;"[48] in their case the confusion is eliminated because the paper is only theoretical, about IR science and two different but related topics: 'discipline' and 'domain of study' and not about international relations of nations and states fifty years ago in which is used 'international relations' in terms of the ad litteram/literally concept and shortening of the information;

(iii) when historians will use in the title and text of their books and articles 'I(i)nternational R(r)elations,' but will specify that the content is not related to the science of IR.

8. As 'science,' 'inter-discipline' and 'specialization,' IR does not have stable research borders.

---

[48] Monterio şi Ruby, "IR and the False Promise," 16.

8.1 In this regard, IR research can be exposed from the point of view of several research interests, which are linked.

8.1.1 (i) *The traditional scope* of IR is to find out about „the causes of war and how to establish the conditions of peace."[49]

8.1.2 (ii) C*auses and solutions*: war, peace, conflict and cooperation.

8.1.3 (iii) *Policies, predictions and forecasts* about the behaviour of nations and states in foreign policy on war, peace, conflict and cooperation.

8.1.4 (iv) *Questions*. E.g.: „How to avoid wars?"[50] and "Why there are no wars between democratic states?"

8.1.4.1 During the research for the traditional scope (which is also a question), other questions related more or less to the traditional scope appeared, but in time they were incorporated into the IR research agenda. Today we can say that some of them have limited/marginalized the traditional scope: "Why some countries are poor

---

[49] See for example: Christian Reus Smith, "International Relations, Irrelevant?," 526.
[50] Frederick S. Dunn, "The Scope of International Relations," *World Politics* 1 (1948): 145, last accessed: December 22, 2012, doi: 10.2307/2009164.

and others are rich?," "Why certain events are presented in a certain way?,"[51] "Can IGOs influence the decisions of the states in the foreign or even in the domestic politics?", or any other questions involving state and non-state actors *and* foreign policy, and, very rarely, domestic politics.

8.1.4.1.1 The IR research of interest for domestic politics exists only when an event, process and phenomenon inside a state is changing because of the external intervention of a second state and this intervention can be made in a peaceful manner (through a share agreement with set and fixed boundaries based on the knowledge in diplomacy or international law), or voluntarily such as military intervention and refusal to respect the sovereignty of the state according with the international law and which can escalate in minutes into an unexpected military conflict.

8.1.4.1.1.1 Here scholars look for the causes of that event, process and phenomenon that was the at the base of the new research interest.

8.1.5 (v) *Processes and daily events*: alliances, treaties, war, peace, conflict, cooperation, economic issues (like stock market, security market, financial crises), problems related to international and European law etc.

---

[51] Goldstein and Pevehouse, *International Relations*, 10-13.

8.1.5.1 Example: Minsk Agreement 2 and the big powers' deal with Iran and Israel's position.

8.1.6 (vi) *Concepts*: power, sovereignty, authority, legitimacy, polarity, terrorism, security (human, national, international, global, economic, environmental), balance of power, war, peace, conflict, cooperation, globalization, global governance, security dilemma, cosmopolitanism etc.[52]

8.1.7 (vii) *Thematic Areas.*

8.1.7.1 Here are some events related to international politics that have changed IR research agenda and brought new thematic area of research: environmental issues (Chernobyl disaster in 1986, United Nations' *Report of the World Commission on Environment and Development: Our Common Future*, 1987[53]), ethnic wars (e.g.: Kosovo and Serbia: 1996 - 1999; the genocide in Rwanda: 7th April - mid June 1994),

---

[52] For a complete list of IR concepts, see Martin Griffiths, Steven C. Roach and M. Scott Solomon, *International Relations: The Key Concepts*, Second Edition, (London, New York: Routledge, 2008).
[53] United Nations, *Report of the World Commission on Environment and Development: Our Common Future*, last accessed: July 10, 2015, http://www.un-documents.net/our-common-future.pdf . Also see the special issue in *International Organization* 26 (1972): 169-478, last accessed: July 10, 2015, http://journals.cambridge.org/action/displayIssue?decade=1970&jid=INO&volumeId=26&issueId=02&iid=3211852

extremist religious groups (e.g.: Al Qaeda, Hamas, Palestinian Islamic Jihad), terrorism (e.g.: Al Qaeda, Hamas, Hezbollah[54]), Internet, the spread of CMNs, TNCs and the emergence of IGOs and thousands of NGOs etc.

8.1.7.1.1 The new IR agenda has as thematic areas: the religion in foreign policy, international economy, foreign trade, economic dependency, foreign aid, social assistance, IGOs', NGOs', CMNs', TNCs' and nations' and states' interest for the environment, terrorism, global financial system, IGOs and NGOs and their influence in the decision of foreign policy and sometimes in domestic politics (like Amnesty International: human rights and Transparency International: corruption), international regimes, security (human, economic, national, international, environmental and so forth), CMNs, TNCs and the development of poor countries, globalization, cooperation, states sovereignty, human rights, organized crime, poverty, foreign interventions, weapons and nuclear weapons proliferation, ethnic minorities, European law, international law etc.[55]

---

[54] "Forbes," *The World's 10 Richest Terrorist Organizations*, last accessed: July 29, 2015,
http://www.forbes.com/sites/forbesinternational/2014/12/12/th e-worlds-10-richest-terrorist-organizations/.
[55] Goldstein and Pevehouse, *International Relations*, 10-13.

8.1.7.1.1.1 This new agenda is used (i) in terms of the research interests from (i) to (vi) and (ii) unrelated to the interests from (i) to (vi).

9. Regarding the **scientific concept** of IR, it refer to those concepts which define IR science, even if the concepts are 'general' or 'particular,' accepted, contested or rejected.

9.1. Due to the existence of several research interests, I think it is impossible to write a universally accepted IR concept. Indeed, by using the ad litteram/literally concept, which I developed in point **4.** + the scope of science + the mode of functioning of inter-discipline, I can form a scientific concept of IR, but my result, even if it is different from other results, is also a general concept, and as such has a reduced analytical use. Here is the result:

„International Relations, shortened IR, by using scientific methods and particular data from at least two disciplines, it studies and researches the links, connections, correspondences, reports between things, facts, ideas, phenomena and processes *between* nations and states and their components/elements, such as: forms of government: monarchy (absolute, constitutional, dualist) or republic (parliamentary, presidential, semi-presidential, directorial, mixed) and theocracy; religion (e.g.: Judaism, Catholicism, Confucianism, Buddhism, Hinduism, Atheism); economics (free, state-controlled, mixed) population (black skin, yellow skin, white skin or Negroid, Mongoloid, Caucasoid also named Europid); culture (e.g.: ways of thinking, values, rules, symbols, clothing, art, music, kitchen); environmental: abiotic (relief, air, water, soil), biotic (plants and animals) and humans (with their activities)."

9.1.1 The result is useless because there is no 'cause', no 'why,' 'no scope for which' we should study and research the relations between nations and states.

9.1.1.1 Here is another example of a general concept written by Joseph Ola:

„International relations are the study of all forms of interactions that exist between members of separate entities or nations within the international system."[56] (Joseph Ola, 1999).

9.1.1.1.1 Both concepts do not have the element of 'particularity' (e.g.: it belongs to a single work or to a single category).[57]

---

[56] Biju Gayu, *Meaning, Nature, Scope and Approaches to International Politics*, April 17, 2012, last accessed: June 20, 2015, http://bijugayu.blogspot.ro/2012/04/meaning-nature-scope-and-approaches-to_17.html#.VdDXb_ntmkp

[57] "particular," Dexonline.ro, last accessed: August 10, 2015, https://dexonline.ro/definitie/particular.

9.1.1.1.1.1 'All relations' and 'all forms of interactions' are general (namely, comprises all) elements of a concept.

9.1.2 Although my concept is scientific and lacks particularity, there are other concepts that have particularity. Here are two examples of IR particular **scientific concept**:

(i) „A discipline, which tries to explain political activities across state borders."[58] (Trevor Taylor, 1979)

(ii) „The discipline of international relations is concerned with the factors and the activities which affect the external policies and power of the basic units into which the world is divided."[59] (Stanley Hoffman)

(iii) The element of particularity in point (i) is the „political activities" and in point (ii) is „the factors and the activities which affect the external policies and power."[60]

10. In points **4.**, **7.** and **9.**, I wrote **A.** two versions of the concept of I(i)nternational R(r)elations: (i) the ad litteram or literally concept and (ii) the scientific concept and **B.** two meanings of the

---

[58] Biju Gayu, *Meaning, Nature, Scope.*
[59] *Ibidem.*
[60] *Ibidem.*

concept I(i)nternational R(r)elations: (i) the general meaning when it is written with lowercase 'international relations' and (ii) and the general meaning when it is written with uppercase 'International Relations,' shortened IR, meaning that I completed a part of the aim of this research. It remains to develop the last aim written in *Introduction*: to build three scientific concepts based on three research interests of the IR 'science,' 'inter-discipline' and 'specialization,' These three concepts eliminate generalization but only from the point of view of the three research interests and concepts.

10.1 I advance three scientific concepts for three out of the seven research interests: (i) *traditional scope*, (ii) *causes and solutions*: war, peace, conflict and cooperation and (iii) *policies, predictions and forecasts* about the behaviour of nations and states in foreign policy on war, peace, conflict and cooperation.

10.1.1 The scientific concept in terms of *the traditional scope*:

„International Relations, shortened IR, using scientific methods and particular data from at least two disciplines, studies and research the links, connections, correspondences, reports between things, facts, ideas, phenomena and processes which are *causes of war and establishes the conditions of peace* between nations and states: forms of government: monarchy (absolute, constitutional, dualist) or republic (parliamentary, presidential, semi-presidential, directorial, mixed) and theocracy; religion (e.g.: Judaism, Catholicism, Confucianism, Buddhism, Hinduism, Atheism); economics (free, state-controlled, mixed); population (black skin, yellow skin, white skin or Negroid, Mongoloid, Caucasoid also named Europid); culture (e.g.: ways of thinking, values, rules, symbols, clothing, art, music, cooking); environment: abiotic (relief, air, water, soil), biotic (plants and animals) and humans (with their activities)."

10.1.2 The scientific concepts in terms of *causes and solutions*:

„International Relations, shortened IR, using scientific methods and particular data from at least two disciplines, it studies and researches the links, connections, correspondences, reports between things, facts, ideas, phenomena and processes which are *causes and solutions* of war, peace, conflict and cooperation between nations and states: forms of government: monarchy (absolute, constitutional, dualist) or republic (parliamentary, presidential, semi-presidential, directorial, mixed) and theocracy; religion (e.g.: Judaism, Catholicism, Confucianism, Buddhism, Hinduism, Atheism); economics (free, state-controlled, mixed) population (black skin, yellow skin, white skin or Negroid, Mongoloid, Caucasoid also named Europid); culture (e.g.: ways of thinking, values, rules, symbols, clothing, art, music, cooking); environmental: abiotic (relief, air, water, soil), biotic (plants and animals) and humans (with their activities)."

10.1.3 The scientific concepts in terms of *policies, predictions and forecasts*:

„International Relations, shortened IR, using scientific methods and particular data from at least two disciplines, studies and researches the links, connections, correspondences, reports between things, facts, ideas, phenomena and processes to create *policies, predictions and forecasts* about the behaviour of the nations and states in foreign policy on war, peace, conflict and cooperation. IR researchers uses data from the components/elements of nations and states: forms of government: monarchy (absolute, constitutional, dualist), republic (parliamentary, presidential, semi-presidential, directorial, mixed) and theocracy; religion (e.g.: Judaism, Catholicism, Confucianism, Buddhism, Hinduism, Atheism); economics (free, state-controlled, mixed) population (black skin, yellow skin, white skin or Negroid, Mongoloid, Caucasoid also named Europid); culture (e.g.: ways of thinking, values, rules, symbols, clothing, art, music, kitchen); environmental: abiotic (relief, air, water, soil), biotic (plants and animals) and humans (with their activities)."

10.1.4 Although do not appear *per se* in the scientific concept, IR studies the relations between nations and states and MNCs, TNCs, IGOs and NGOs from the point of view of the seven IR research interests.

10.1.4.1 MNCs, TNCs, IGOs and NGOs are *inside* the concept, more precisely, in the elements of the scientific concept and based on their activity: politics, economics, religion and so forth.

11. To find the answers to IR research agenda, IR researchers combine, merge, bring research methodologies, concepts, bodies of knowledge, thinking patterns, ideas and particular data from at least two disciplines: history (especially the history of diplomacy), geography, political studies (theories, ideologies and concepts), economics (e.g.: market), demography, anthropology (e.g.: cultural system of the people), psychology (e.g.: personality, public opinion, propaganda, masses' emotions), sociology (e.g.: social behaviour), environment: abiotic (relief, air, water, soil), biotic (plants and animals) and humans (with their activities).[61]

---

[61] Waldermar Gurian, "On the Study of International Relations," *The Review of Politics* 8 (1946): 277, last accessed: February 15, 2015, doi: 10.1017/S0034670500040857; Harold D. Lasswell, "Some Reflections on the Study of International Relations," *World Politics* 8 (1956): 560-565, last accessed: July 17, 2014, doi: 10.2307/2008945; Chris Brown, "The Future of the Discipline?," *International Relations* 21(2007): 350, doi: 10.1177/0047117807082713; Brian C. Schmidt, "On the History and Historiography of International Relations," in *Handbook of International Relations* ed. Walter Carlsnaes, Thomas Risse and Beth A. Simmons, (London: Sage Publication, 2012): 6.

11.1 Based on the results obtained with the help of many disciplines, IR researchers formulate theories, laws, comments, analyses, research notes, scientific essays, opinions, policies, forecasting and predictions.

11.1.1 Among theories, I mention: realism, liberalism, postmodernism, constructivism, feminism, English school, critic theory, international political theory/international ethics, historical sociology etc.[62]

11.2 The fact that particular data is combined with other particular data from at least two disciplines, in IR:

(i) there is no consensus among researchers on IR as 'integral science' in the 'social sciences;'[63]

(ii) does not have a coherent theoretical identity;

(iii) there are problems with the conceptual and theoretical approaches;

---

[62] It is based on Martin Griffiths, Steven C. Roach and M. Scott Solomon, *Fifty Key Thinkers in International Relations Theory*, First Edition, (London, New York: Routledge, 1999) and Martin Griffiths, Steven C. Roach and M. Scott Solomon, *Fifty Key Thinkers in International Relations Theory*, Second Edition, (London, New York: Routledge, 2009).
[63] Monterio and Ruby, *"IR and the False Promise,"* 15-48.

(iv) has a body of knowledge, theories, laws, concepts and thinking patterns discovered and proposed after using particular data from other disciplines, but which are not enough to make a 'discipline;'

(v) has a professional discourse;[64]

(vi) there are debates, books, journals, meetings, universities, IR associations.[65]

12. The roots of IR inter-discipline, from the point of view of the traditional scope, with regard to war and peace, are found in books written by Sun Tzu,[66] Thucydides,[67] Niccolò Machiavelli,[68]

---

[64] Brian Schmidt, *"History and Historiography,"* 5.

[65] *Ibidem*, 3.

[66] Sun Tzu, *The Art of War*, last accessed: July 4, 2015, http://classics.mit.edu/Tzu/artwar.html.

[67] Thucydides, *History of the Peloponnesian War*, 431 B.C.E., last accessed: July 4, 2015,http://www.gutenberg.org/ebooks/7142.

[68] Niccolò Machiavelli, *The Prince*, (1513), last accessed: July 4, 2015,http://www.gutenberg.org/ebooks/1232.

Thomas Hobbes,[69] Hugo Grotius,[70] Adam Smith,[71] Jean-Jacques Rousseau,[72] and many others.

12.1 To be more accurate, IR researchers continue and apply their research.

12.1.1 Interest for the causes of war intensified immediately after the First World War.

12.1.1.1 Idealism (e.g.: Norman Angell, Alfred Zimmern) appears as a reaction to realism that led to the First World War.[73] During and after the Second World War, the realism (e.g. E.H. Carr, Hans Morgenthau) appears as a reaction to

---

[69] Thomas Hobbes, *Leviathan*, (1651), last accessed: July 4, 2015,https://archive.org/details/leviathan03207gut.

[70] Hugo Grotius, *On the Law of War and Peace*, (1625), last accessed: July 4, 2015,http://www.constitution.org/gro/djbp.htm.

[71] Adam Smith, *An Inquiry into the Nature and Causes of the Wealth of Nations*, (1776), last accessed: July 4, 2015,http://www.econlib.org/library/Smith/smWN.html.

[72] Jean-Jacques Rousseau, *The Social Contract Or Principles of Political Right,* (1762), last accessed: July 4, 2015, https://www.marxists.org/reference/subject/economics/rousseau /social-contract/index.htm, electronic edition.

[73] „[...] John Vasquez wrote: „that the first stage of international relations inquiry was dominated by the idealist paradigm," which he claims was „important in terms of institutionalizing the field and creating the emphasis on peace and war [...]"" in Brian C. Schmidt, "Anarchy, World Politics and the Birth of a Discipline: American International Relations, Pluralist Theory and the Myth of Interwar Idealism," *International Relations* 16 (2002): 11, last accessed: February 24, 2015, doi: 10.1177/0047117802016001003.

idealism that brought Second World War.[74] The end of the Second World War and the new non state actors like the United Nations, European Coal and Steel Community (today the European Union), United Nations Educational, Scientific and Cultural Organization (UNESCO), The Arab League, World Bank, North Atlantic Organization (NATO), International Monetary Fund (IMF) brought new theories, strengthen the current ones or new theories appeared about war, peace, conflicts and cooperation: the institutionalized neo-liberalism (e.g.: Robert Keohane, Jospeh Nye), neo-realism (e.g.: Kenneth T. Waltz), radical theories (e.g.: Robert Cox, Andrew Linklater), green theory, English school (e.g.: Barry Buzan, Hedley Bull, Martin Wight) etc. The Cold War brought constructivism (e.g.: Friedrich Kratochwil, John Gerard Ruggie, Christian Reus-Smit, Alexander Wendt), postmodernism (e.g.: Richard Ashley, Michel Foucault) and other papers which strengthen or add something new to all the above mentioned theories.[75]

12.1.1.1.1 All theories have emerged as a response to the international political life.

---

[74] Kenneth W. Thompson, "Idealism and Realism: Beyond the Great Debate," *British Journal of International Studies* 3 (1977): 199-209, last accessed: July, 9 2015, doi: 10.1017/S0260210500116997.
[75] The complete list of theories and thinkers see Griffiths, Roach and Solomon, *Fifty Key Thinkers*, first and second edition.

12.1.1.1.1.1 The life of the international politics is created by events within national states; it is a side effect that can endanger other states, which leads to a chain reaction and, therefore, the creation of the life of international politics (positive and negative).

12.2 From the point of view of the traditional scope, in the last century, IR researchers have produced a deep and new knowledge but not final about the causes of war and the conditions of peace: Hans J. Morgenthau, *Politics Among Nations, The Struggle for Power and Peace*, Seventh Edition, (New York: McGraw-Hill Education, 2005); A. F. K. Organski, *World Politics*, Second Edition, (New York: Alfred A. Knopf, 1968); Robert Gilpin, *The Political Economy of International Relations*, (Princeton: Princeton University Press, 1987) and *Global Political Economy - Understanding the International Economic Order*, (Princeton: Princeton University Press, 2001); Geoffrey Blainey, *The Causes of War*, Third Edition (New York: Free Press, 1988), Stephen Van Evera, *Causes of War. Power and the Roots of Conflict*, (Ithaca, London: Cornell University Press, 1999) and Jack S. Levi and William R. Thompson, *Causes of War*, (London: Wiley-Blackwell, 2010).

12.3 As regarding the other six research interests, here there is a new and deep knowledge too.

13. The beginning of IR as academic inter-discipline is associated with the first *Department of International Politics*, University College of Wales (at present Aberystwyth University), Great Britain, 1919.

13.1 David Davis was born on May 11, 1880, Llandinam, Montgomeryshire, Great Britain.

13.1.1 He was a liberal, a man of idealism ideas, active supporter of the United Nations and of a world government.[76]

13.1.2 In the First World War, David Davies was a battalion commander. Soon after the war, with his sisters Margaret and Gwendoline Davies, donated the amount of £ 20,000 in the memory of the dead and injured students to the University College of Wales (at present Aberystwyth University), for founding a *Department of International Politics* in order to study international politics with emphasis on the promotion of peace between nations and states.[77]

---

[76] Brian Porter, "Lord Davies, E.H. Carr and the Spirit Ironic: a Comedy of Errors," *International Relations* 16 (2002): 81, last accessed: July 15, 2012, doi: 10.1177/0047117802016001006.
[77] Brian Porter, *"Lord Davis,"* 78; Brian Schmidt, *"History and Historiography,"* 4; Ken Booth, "The Writing on the Way," *International Relations* 21 (2007): 360, last accessed: February 24, 2015, doi: 10.1177/0047117807080213.

13.1.2.1 After the founding of this department, other universities have appeared with a *Department of Politics and International Relation*s. Here are two examples:

(i) *Edmund A. Walsh School of Foreign Service* (1919) from Georgetown University, USA.

(ii) *Graduate Institute of International and Development Studies* (1927) known as the *Institut de Hautes Études Internationales et du Développement* or *Graduate Institute Geneva*, Switzerland.

14. As regarding the abolition of war, in 1910, Andrew Carnegie funded this cause.

14.1 Andrew Carnegie (November 25, 1835 - August 11, 1919) was a Scottish-origin living-in-America businessman and philanthropist.

14.2 During his life, he participated in numerous conferences and meetings and wrote many articles about war and world peace:[78]

Andrew Carnegie: "The Washington Arbitration Conference," *The Advocate of Peace (1894-1920)*

---

[78] Andrew Carnegie, "The Path to Peace," *The Advocate for Peace* 73 (1911): 184, last accessed: June 26, 2015, http://www.jstor.org/stable/20665780?seq=1#page_scan_tab_contents.

58 (1896): 110-124; "The Venezuelan Question," *The North American Review* 162 (1896): 129-144; "The South African Question," *The North American Review* 169 (1899): 798-804 "Letter of Andrew Carnegie to the Peace Congress, " *The Advocate of Peace (1894-1920)* 66 (1904): 233; "Peace to Come at Last — A Peace League of the Nations," *The Advocate of Peace (1894-1920)* 67 (1905): 247-254; "The Wrong Path," *The Advocate of Peace (1894-1920)* 71 (1909): 103-105; "Armaments and Their Results," *The Advocate of Peace (1894-1920)* 71, (1909): 211-221; "War as the Mother of Valor and Civilization," *The Advocate of Peace (1894-1920)* 72 (1910): 82-83; "The Result of the Arbitration Treaty. From the Contemporary Review, August, 1911," *The Advocate of Peace (1894-1920)* 73 (1911): 278; "The Baseless Fear of War," *The Advocate of Peace (1894-1920)* 75 (1913): 79-80; "The Moral Issue Involved in War," *The Advocate for Peace* (1984-1920) 73 (1911): 34-36. A part of Andrew Carnegie papers are available for free, online, on JSTOR.[79]

14.3 In December 1910, in a room from *Carnegie Research Foundation*, Washington, United States, Andrew Carnegie announced the establishment of

---

[79] Here is this link: http://www.jstor.org/action/doBasicResults?group=none&wc=off &fc=off&Query=au:%22Andrew+Carnegie%22&hp=100&acc=off& so=old&si=1 (last accessed: June 20, 2015).

a fund to be used to „hasten the abolition of international war and establish peace:"[80]

„Gentlemen: I have transferred to you as trustees of the Carnegie Peace Fund ten millions of five per cent, first mortgage bonds, worth of eleven and a half million of dollars, revenue of which is to be administered by you to hasten the abolition of international war, the foulest blot upon our civilization."[81]

14.3.1 Following his donations, the *Carnegie Endowment for International Peace* was founded and is highly involved in the science of International Relations and contributed with an extensive knowledge.

14.3.2 In the next year, 1911, the *Carnegie Endowment for International Peace* has come with a report which said that:

„as a prerequisite for ridding the world of war, solid knowledge was required on „the underlying forces which move nations, the development of their

---

[80] "Ten Millions for Peace," *The Advocate of Peace* 73 (1911): 1-2, last accessed: July 18, 2015, http://www.jstor.org/stable/20666089?seq=1#page_scan_tab_contents.
[81] "Andrew Carnegie's Announcement of His Great Peace Fund," *The Advocate of Peace* 73 (1911): 7, last accessed: December 2012, http://www.jstor.org/stable/20666096?seq=1#page_scan_tab_contents.

methods and motives of action and the historical development of their relations.""[82]

15. In point **1.** and **2.** I explored the terms 'relation' and 'international.' At the level of the use of the two terms under a single formula 'international relations,' from my research, it appeared in articles published in journals about foreign and domestic policy of nations and states, before the development of IR as a science, inter-discipline and academic specialization.

15.1 Here are three articles with 'International Relations:'

(i) Albert Bushnell Hart, "American Ideals of International Relations," *The American Journal of International Law* 1 (1907): 624-635, accessed February 15, 2015, http://www.jstor.org/stable/2186822;

(ii) George W. Nasmyth, "The Universities and American International Relations," *The Journal of Race Development* 5 (1914): 98-104, accessed February 15, 2015, http://www.jstor.org/stable/29738027;

---

[82] Harry Howe Rasom, "International Relations," *The Journal of Politics* 30 (1968): 345, last accessed: February 15, 2015, http://www.jstor.org/stable/2128446?seq=1#page_scan_tab_contents.

(iii) Benoy Kumar Sarkar, "Hindu Theory of International Relations," *The American Political Science Review* 13 (1919): 400-414, accessed February 15, 2015, http://www.jstor.org/stable/1945958.

15.2 As regarding the term 'international' in articles' title from journals, it was used long before 'International Relations.' Here are two examples:

(i) Francis Fellowes, "The Progress of International Law in Reference to the Objects of Peace Societies," *American Advocate of Peace (1834-1836)* 1, (1834): 33-47, accessed February 15, 2015, http://www.jstor.org/stable/pdf/27886762.pdf;

(ii) Francis Fellowes, "War as a Mean of International Justice," *American Advocate of Peace (1834-1836)* 1 (1834): 64-72, accessed February 15, 2015, http://www.jstor.org/stable/27886773.

15.3 There are also journals that have written prior to the development of International Relations as 'science,' 'inter-discipline' and 'specialization' about relations between nations and states, just as it occurs today, but with the problems at that time.

15.3.1 1834 is the year in which appeared the first root of a journal that will become one of the best in IR. It is the journal named *The American Advocate for Peace*. Here is the historical evolution and changes of name:

(i) *American Advocate for Peace* (1834-1837);[83]

(ii) *The Advocate of Peace* (1837-1845);[84]

(iii) *The Advocate of Peace and Universal Brotherhood* (1846);[85]

(iv) *Advocate of Peace* (1847-1884);[86]

(v) *The American Advocate of Peace and Arbitration* (1889-1892);[87]

(vi) *American Advocate of Peace* (1892-1893);[88]

(vii) *The Advocate of Peace* (1894-1920);[89]

---

[83] "American Advocate for Peace" (1834-1837),
http://www.jstor.org/journal/advopeace1834.
[84] "The Advocate of Peace" (1837-1845),
http://www.jstor.org/journal/advopeace1837.
[85] "The Advocate of Peace and Universal Brotherhood" (1846),
http://www.jstor.org/journal/advopeacunivbro.
[86] "Advocate of Peace" (1847-1884),
http://www.jstor.org/journal/advopeace1847.
[87] "The American Advocate of Peace and Arbitration" (1889-1892),
http://www.jstor.org/journal/amadvopeacarbi.
[88] "American Advocate of Peace" (1892-1893),
http://www.jstor.org/journal/amadvopeace.
[89] "The Advocate of Peace" (1894-1920),
http://www.jstor.org/journal/advopeac1894.

viii) *Advocate of Peace through Justice* (1920-1932);[90]

(ix) *World Affairs* (1932-present).[91]

15.3.2 In 1910, another journal was published but with articles more focused in the area of IR: *The Journal of Race Development.*

15.3.2.1 Although the name suggests eugenics (a theory of expected improvement that human populations may achieve through genetic measures – choosing the parents, sterilization, prohibition of procreation of those people with weak gens etc.), the journal focused on topics such as government, education, religion, industry and social conditions. The races and states most frequently discussed were India, the Near East, Africa and the Far East, except for Japan.[92] Here is the historical evolution and the changes of names:

---

[90] "Advocate of Peace through Justice" (1920-1932), http://www.jstor.org/journal/advopeacjust.
[91] "World Affairs (1932-present), http://www.jstor.org/journal/worldaffairs, http://www.worldaffairsjournal.org/.
[92] George H. Blakeslee, "Introduction," *The Journal of Race Development* 1 (1910): 1, last accessed: July 14, 2015, http://www.jstor.org/stable/pdf/29737842.pdf.

(i) *The Journal of Race Development* (1910-1919);[93]

(ii) *The Journal of International Relations* (1919-1922) - the first journal in the world with the name of the inter-discipline;[94]

(iii) *Foreign Affairs* (1922-present). *The Journal of International Relations* entered in the newly established heritage of the *Council of Foreign Relations* (1922), which decided to change the name in *Foreign Affairs*.[95]

15.3.3 The journal *Political Science Quarterly* (1866-present) had a supplement number with many sections, one of them with the title 'International Relations.' Here are the first tree and the last number of the journal IR sections:

(i) volume 31, no. 3, 1916: http://www.jstor.org/stable/i3112031916 (last accessed: July 21, 2015);

---

[93] "The Journal of Race Development" (1910-1919), http://www.jstor.org/journal/jracedeve.
[94] "The Journal of International Relations" (1919-1922), http://www.jstor.org/journal/jinterelations.
[95] "Foreign Affairs" (1922-present), http://www.jstor.org/journal/foreignaffairs, https://www.foreignaffairs.com/.

(ii) volume 32, no. 3, 1917:
http://www.jstor.org/stable/i311208 (last accessed: July 21, 2015);

(iii) volume 33, no. 3, 1918:
http://www.jstor.org/stable/i311213 (last accessed: July 21, 2015);

(iv) volume 40, no. 1, 1925:
http://www.jstor.org/stable/i311244 (last accessed: July 21, 2015).

15.3.4 Other important journal from IR, but only with 'International:'

(i) *Journal of the British Institute of International Affairs* (1922-1926);[96]

(ii) *Journal of the Royal Institute of International Affairs* (1926-1930);[97]

(iii) *International Affairs* (Royal Institute of International Affairs 1931-1939);[98]

---

[96] "Journal of the British Institute of International Affairs" (1922-1926), http://www.jstor.org/journal/jbritinstinteaff.
[97] "Journal of the Royal Institute of International Affairs" (1926-1930), http://www.jstor.org/journal/jroyainstinteaff.
[98] "International Affairs (Royal Institute of International Affairs" 1931-1939), http://www.jstor.org/journal/inteaffaroyains2.

(iv) *International Affairs Review Supplement* (1940-1943);[99]

(v) *International Affairs* (Royal Institute of International Affairs 1944-present).[100]

---

[99] "International Affairs Review Supplement" (1940-1943), http://www.jstor.org/journal/inteaffarevisupp.
[100] "International Affairs (Royal Institute of International Affairs" (1944-present), http://www.jstor.org/journal/inteaffaroyainst.

CONCLUSIONS

1. In this paper I explored the concept of I(i) international R(r)elations: two versions of the concept I(i) international R(r)elations: (i) the ad litteram or literally concept and (ii) the scientific concept; two meanings of the concept of I(i) international relations: (i) the general meaning when it is written in lower case international relations and (ii) the general meaning when it is written in capital letters International Relations, abbreviated RI.

1.1 In short, the writing techniques have the following meaning:

(i) when we find it written with lowercase 'international relations' = in general it refers to the ad litteram/literally concept; shortens the information;

(ii) when we find it written with uppercase 'International Relations' (abbreviated IR) = in general it refers to 'science' (the scientific concept), 'inter-discipline' and 'specialization' of IR.

2. Although there are two techniques of writing, (i) there is a situation where an author uses 'international relations' and refers to discipline and science, but each time there is an explanation that it is written in the introduction of the book or article; (ii) there is a situation where an author uses one of the version of the concept 'I(i)international R(r)elations' without providing any explanation of the concept, but it is understood from the text that it is an ad litteram concept and not about the discipline and the science of IR.

3. The path and process of creating a concept is not easy, but this paper provided a good reference point to show how the concept of 'International Relations' is created: from what sources it starts and how ends up being used in practice.

Endnotes

1. The sources from notes *2, 3, 4, 5, 17, 18, 19, 20, 21, 22, 23, 24, 26, 27, 30, 31, 32, 33, 34, 35, 60* and *61* were accessed on February 2015, but I used the last date on which they were accessed in order to verify the existence of the internet page.

1.1 The remaining sources were accessed on the date mentioned.

1.2 Some sources contain a link, but not the date of access: those online sources are stable and do not change the access link.

Author note:

Thank you for taking the time to read this short book.

On the Famous Feud (2022): In this report I investigated the *Famous* feud between Kim Kardashian, Kanye West and Taylor Swift. The mechanisms for interpreting the feud are multiple and there is still a great interest in debating the perpetrators and the victims of the feud. This report was born out of the urgent need to provide clearer, more transparent information and better-founded examples to explain the feud for the general public in a different way than what Kim Kardashian, Kanye West and Taylor Swift offered through music, interviews and other media content. This report exposes the background strategies of Kanye West, Kim Kardashian, Taylor Swift and Western mass-media to maintain popularity and fame in an ever-changing world: sacrifices, intelligence, methods of communications, side effects and a minimal view of the efficiency of their strategies in the long term.

Black and White Music: A Journey Behind the Musical Notes (2022): In this report I explored a very small part of the music industry from the USA, more precisely, I investigated the contribution, greater or lesser, of black and white artists in the production and writing of their albums. The artists investigated in this report are Taylor Swift, Kanye West, Beyoncé, Kendrick Lamar, Macklemore & Ryan, Adele and Beck. I selected these artists because the music produced and released by them were used by various artists and journalists as examples of racial discrimination that takes place in the music industry. In other words, today's music industry is caught in a difficult situation that is severely undermining The Recording Academy's credibility and the Grammy Awards.

The full experience of *Revi Project 88* is available online:

Printed in Poland
by Amazon Fulfillment
Poland Sp. z o.o., Wrocław

11511088R00040